"Healing medicine spoken gracefully

God's Words
Plain and Simple

Rayna Stephens

Formerly Rayna Roxanne

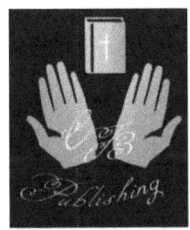

CJ3 Publishing LLC
2330 Scenic Highway, Ste 503
Snellville, GA 30078

©2019 Rayna Stephens. All rights Reserved.

No part of this book may be reproduced, stored in a retrieval system, or transmitted by any means without the written permission of the author. Revised and Published by CJ3 Publishing LLC 10/15/2019

ISBN: 978-0-578-58010-4 (sc)
ISBN: 978-0-578-58011-1 (e)

Library of Congress Control Number: 2011917696
Printed in the United States of America
Illustrations by Jamon Stephens
All imagery in this book is original ©Rayna Stephens

Because of the dynamic nature of the Internet, any web addresses or links contained in this book may have changed since publication and may no longer be valid. The views expressed in this work are solely those of the author and do not necessarily reflect the views of the publisher, and the publisher hereby disclaims any responsibility for them.

ACKNOWLEDGMENTS

I would like to thank God for graciously giving, to me, the gift of writing. I know it has come from Him and no one else, and I could not have done it without him. I would also like to thank my beautiful children, Chantrelle, Jamon, Anthony Jr. and Jarren; and my grandson, Markel for enduring all the trying times we have had together. I praise God that He has given me such strong and faithful children. They could have turned to the world, instead, they held on to their faith, in God, and stuck it out with momma; and I love them for that. You all are very dear to my heart and I want to, humbly, say thank you.

I want to show my appreciation to those who have encouraged and inspired me thru this journey, as well; Reverend Brian Lipscomb, Ms. Annett Everett, Andrea Watson-Harris, Mrs. Ercille Devine, Bethany Devine, Sister Mary Woods, Camille Pollard; and last but not least, my mother, Opaline Lynn, my sister, Dana Stephens and all of my family and friends. It is truly a blessing to have such wonderful sisters and brothers in Christ supporting me every step of the way. May God keep and bless you in everything you do, according to his will!

With the love of Christ,

Ray

Contents

Acknowledgments 1

Jesus: The Maintenance Man 5

Supernatural Being 6

Tag Team Partner 7

His Worth 9

A Child's Prayer 12

When A Sinner Pray 14

Lost But Found 15

You Prayed Me Thru 17

Redeemed 19

Broken 22

Change 24

A Poem for Gabriel 25

A Sober Soul 28

Identity Crisis 30

Come unto Me 32

He will Deliver You 33

The Visit 34

From Satan's Playpen Back to the Garden of Eden 37

Happy "Birth"Day 40

Living in the Paradise of God's Character 42

I've Been Kept 44

Who I Am 46

True "Model of Beauty" 47

Friend 49

My Compliment 50
A Kingdom Man 51
Missing Rib 53
A Kingdom Woman 55
I'm Ready 57
Have Your Way 59
Persevere 62
Stepping into My Destiny 63
On the Outside Trying to Look In 65
Confidence In Christ 67
I Won With a Bad Hand 69
Faithfulness in My Faith 71
Worship 74
A Balm Thru the Storm 77
FEAR into FAITH 79
I Believe 81
Faith Walk 82
About the Author 84
A Poem for the Youth 87
My Mother 89
Order Information 90

Rayna Stephens

JESUS: THE MAINTENANCE MAN

JESUS is:
A massage to my soul when it's weary
A healing medicine when I am sick
A stress reliever when I am burnt out
A burden bearer when I am worried
A peace in the middle of my storm
A light in darkness when I can not see
A reassurance when I am in doubt
A sustainer when I need to be kept
A provider when I am in need
A protector when I am in danger
A refuge when I am in need of shelter
A comforter when I am lonely
A friend when I need someone to confide in
A father when I need a daddy's advice
A mother when I need a tender touch
Joy when I am in sorrow
Strength in the time of my weakness
Grace when I am in need of favor
Mercy when I am in need of forgiveness
Wisdom when I am in need of knowledge
Faith when I am in need of hope
Discipline when I am in need of correction
A Savior when I am in need of redemption
Love and compassion when I feel hated by others

JESUS is: The Maintenance Man

March 20, 2010

Rayna Stephens

SUPERNATURAL BEING

I was once asked the question, does God really exist
And my answer was, yes, He's a supernatural
being who is here to assist

I have heard scholars of science say an
answer like mine could be debated
But what they should realize is He was always
here; even before the world was created

He's the 'One' who created the heavens and the
earth, and everything within, in six days
He's the 'One' who performs supernatural miracles
in our lives that leave all of us amazed

He's the 'One' who calms our spirit when we can't
take the pain; when we're about to explode
He's called the comforter for a reason; He's the
only 'One' who can soothe our aching souls

He's the 'One' who saves us when we
have condemned ourselves to hell
He's the 'One' who manifests the Holy Spirit
within us so we may have a story to tell

He's the 'One' who wills us to have genuine
faith; believing in the unseen
Because He is God; and God all by
Himself, the Supernatural Being

03/26/2010

TAG TEAM PARTNER

Inspired by, my son, Anthony Jr.

You said that you are the true vine and
your Father is the gardener,
So Jesus, I'm up against a fight and I need
you to be my tag team partner.

I know you will keep me
regardless of the matter,
The crowd is already here, so I
need you to fight this battle.

They are watching me, closely, to
see if I will stand or fall,
They are watching my reactions
when my back is against the wall.

They are wondering how I can stand the
kicks and punches of the enemy,
But they failed to see that I tagged you in; and
you are standing directly in front of me.

You told me to hang in there because
the fight was almost over,
You told me you were going to step aside and
allow the enemy to come a little closer.

You said you will use me this way to
Show the worldly crowd your powers,
You will show them that you are their
protector every night, day and hour.

Rayna Stephens

The devil thought he had me; thought
he was really clever,
But, God, you said, when you act, out
of your hand, who can deliver?

The bell has rang, the fight is over and I
have stumbled; where will I land?
Wow! I opened my eyes and was the winner because I
was still standing in my Master's most powerful hand!

December 6, 2010

HIS WORTH

The sound of the wind rush thru the trees,
against the pane of my window
The raindrops falling from the heavens as
a curtain closing on a stage show

The sounds of the birds' graceful and
innocent harmonized chirps
These sounds are of God's whispers
and recognitions of **His Worth**

I trust you, oh Lord, wholeheartedly,
I trust you like never before
I trust that you will not let me walk
outside of your Holy will anymore

Your faithfulness, kindness, strength,
compassion and your love
I know these qualities you give to me
only come from Heaven above

You speak to me in the quietest spirit,
. blessing my ears to be inclined
With your power, you speak words of wisdom
into my confused earthly mind

The authority of your precious voice is
extremely strong, yet small and gentle
I feel cuddled in your arms with no cares
in the world, not even a little

Rayna Stephens

      I believe what you say to me will be
    accomplished, and now the time is here
      If I just keep the faith, don't give up,
        hold on and continue to persevere

    You are my priest, my protector, and
       my provider in my times of need
    Thank you, Lord, for sustaining me, and
    with my soul, I'll bless your name indeed

     I'll honor you, glorify you, praise you
     And worship you to the ends of the earth
Because, I've learned to recognize the sounds of
your whispers and the beauty of **Your Worth!**

May 24, 2009

God's Words

Rayna Stephens

A Child's Prayer

Ok, so if there really is a God
and you are real as people say,
Then, tonight I want to talk with you
so I'll get down on my knees to pray.

I want to know why I go thru so much
hurt, pain and abuse; I'm just a child,
Why can't I have a normal life like other
children? Why can't I live each day with a smile?

Why do I have to take care of my
Siblings as if I'm their father or mother?
When I am in need just as they are; I'm
only their big sister or brother.

Why do I have to be a victim of
poverty, abuse, molestation and rape?
If you are really God and can hear me, I pray
for a way out of this life; a way to escape.

Why do I do things I know I shouldn't
do, just to get my parent's attention?
Yet and still it didn't work and now I'm
entrapped in this facility called detention.

Why do they say, "I work hard, sometimes
two jobs, to give you everything you've got?"
When they don't realize everything doesn't
matter, I desire their love and time; I need it a lot.

God's Words

I was told to pray and believe, then receive
if, in my life, I wanted and desired a change,
I was told to call on your Son, Jesus, so I
may be saved, by your grace, thru His name.

Jesus, I'm calling on you, I'm about to give
up, I need you to come to rescue me right now
I'll believe my life is about to change for the
good, and you will do it for me, somehow.

I'm going to say thank you, in
advance, for what is about to be done,
And I will believe I'm already delivered
and the victory I have already won.

03/20/2010

Rayna Stephens

WHEN A SINNER PRAY

When a sinner pray, the doors
and windows of Heaven open up
God's ears and heart have become
attentive so he may fill the sinner's cup

When a sinner pray, satan becomes
shaken up, distorted, scared and confused
He knows when God hears a sinner's prayer,
it is one more soul that he is about to lose

When a sinner pray, he is setting himself
up to be redeemed by the Lord above
He has come back to the 'One' that he
knows, for a fact, will show him love

When a sinner pray, Heaven rejoices
And there is nothing satan can do or say
Because God is always there, ready and
willing to save, when a sinner pray

March 15, 2010

God's Words

LOST BUT FOUND

Inspired by, my son, Jarren

I remember the day when I was lost; my
world was spinning round and round
But, I also remember the day when I accepted
Jesus, with all my heart, then, I was found

When I was lost, I felt like a helpless child,
standing in the midst of a busy one-way street
But when I was found, my soul felt a covering
that was more gentle than a baby's sheet

When I was lost, I only cared about me
and what I could accomplish only for myself
But when I was found, God restored, in me,
selflessness so I may care for someone else

When I was lost, I desired the things that were
offered to me by the prince of this corrupt world
But when I was found, I desired the kingdom of
Heaven; I was no longer a materialistic guy or girl

When I was lost, satan deceived me into thinking
my trials were permanent; this was my life
But when I was found, I realized prayer with faith
changed things and I could have a better life in Christ

When I was lost and lived life in the world, my
"so-called" friends were always hanging around
But, when I was found, they scattered like
roaches and could not be found thru-out the town

Rayna Stephens

When I was lost, my burdens were heavy; I
became depressed and wanted to lie down and die
But when I was found, those same burdens were
lifted, and out of my spirit flowed a joyful cry

When I was lost, the road to my life's journey
was blurred; I was blinded and could not see
But when I was found, God reminded me when I
walked thru the valley that he was carrying me

When I was lost, I was a liar, a cheat, and a
deceiver; I was condemned from any good
But when I was found, Jesus created, in
me, a new spirit just as he said he would

When I was lost, my soul was condemned to
the pits of hell; I thought I would never be found
But when I was found, God saved me by his amazing
grace; and nothing could ever be sweeter than that sound!

April 4, 2010

You Prayed Me Thru

Dedicated to Mrs. Ercille Devine

You prayed for me from the first time we met
Having you in my life could never be a regret

You prayed for me when I couldn't pray for myself
You asked Him to cover me and be my everlasting help

You prayed for me when I
felt I couldn't be restrained
You asked that even thru my
ignorance He would keep me sustained

You prayed for me when I didn't
think I was a good mother
You asked for strength and grace that
only came from God and no other

You prayed for me when I lost all
hope and was about to give up
You asked that with goodness
and mercy may He fill my cup

You prayed for me while I was
in the world, lost and confused
You asked for wisdom that I give
my life to Him so that I may be used

Rayna Stephens

You prayed for me and never gave up on
me, and for that, I want to thank you
Because it was by your prayers and His
grace that Jesus kept and saw me safely thru
You prayed me thru and I love you for that; I really do

October 26, 2009

REDEEMED

The precious future the Lord had
for me, I could not physically see
So I closed my eyes, stepped out on
faith and allowed him to guide me

I would sulk in my tears, doubting the
impossible yet hoping for a change
When the entire time, Jesus was right
there telling me to ask in his name

So I did what He said; I asked in his
name; praising and ready to receive
But there was a step I had a problem
with; with all my heart I did not believe

He said to me, "Once again, I will allow
you to go thru this unnecessary process"
"You'll go back thru the hurt, the pain,
the confusion and all the other mess"

He did just what he said; and I lived in
misery until I couldn't take it anymore
I fell to my knees, in tears, calling on the name
of Jesus as if I were banging on Heaven's door

He allowed me to bang for quite a
while; until I was totally sincere
Then he grabbed my spirit and held it close
and said, "I never left you, I was always near."

Rayna Stephens

He said, "I had to this challenging
and unwanted process
Because, I have something much greater
for you and I need you to be at your best."

So I humbled myself as his vessel
and gave over, to him, my life
"Use me Lord," I said, "the way you want; I
know with you everything will be alright"

He said, "ok daughter, I will do so; but for
You I have a task and it will cause a flood"
And he said, "don't worry, my child, because
you are already covered under my blood"

I said, "Ok Lord, here **we** go; I'm stepping out
on your word and my faith, no more guessing"
He said, "You did not have to guess, and for
being obedient, here comes your mighty blessings"

So to those who are lost and think
there is absolutely no help for you
Try my Jesus! You can't go wrong; I know
for a fact he will safely carry you thru

As a witness of being in the Lord's
presence, I am able to tell you this story
Don't get it twisted, I take no credit;
It's all for my God's glory!

April 1, 2009

God's Words

Rayna Stephens

BROKEN

Break me, Lord Jesus, break me, please; I want to break
Break me in a way so, by you, I may be saved
Saved by your precious mercy and grace
So I may have the strength to run this race
And when this life is over, I may live with you face to face.

Break me, Lord Jesus, please; I desire to be broken up
So you can melt me, mend me, shape me and then fill my cup
Fill me with your wisdom, discernment, peace, joy and love
So I may stand the test to tell the world you are really what's up
The God who sits on the throne in the Heaven's above
So your children will see there's reassurance if they only look up.

Break me, Lord Jesus, please; I want to be transformed
I surrender my spirit to you and I want to be conformed
So in my life, by your powers, your Holy will may be performed
And others may believe you can keep them in their storms
So they may humble themselves and they too can be conformed
To tell the world about your glory and we all may be reformed.

Break me, Lord Jesus, please; I desire to live a better life
Not just of materialistic blessings, but a better life in Christ
A life that can withstand the trials, tests, temptations and strife
A practice of my faith and obedience so I may gain eternal life
And to help others draw closer to you and be saved by our Savior,
Jesus Christ

God's Words

So break me, Lord Jesus, break me please; I want to break
Break me in a way, Lord Jesus, that I may be saved
Saved by your precious mercy and grace
So I may have the strength to run this race
And when this life is over, I may dwell with
you, forever, face to face

November 5, 2009

Rayna Stephens

CHANGE

Dear God,
Change my:
Fears into courage
Doubts into reassurance
Frustrations into determination
Ignorance into wisdom
Stress into strength
Selfishness into selflessness
Depression into joy
Transgressions into sanctification
Lies into truth
Greed into giving
Racism into brotherhood
Laziness into laboring
Aggression into humbleness
Anger into temperance
Rebellion into obedience
Disrespect into honor
Trials into testimonies
Hatred into love
Failures into victory
Lost spirit into a saved soul
In Jesus Name,
Amen

October 22, 2009

A Poem for Gabriel

Dedicated to Gabriel Jones

Lord, I'm in a place that
is not familiar to me
I need your help to guide me
back to where I should be

I have done some things in my life
I know I should not have done
But I have given my life back to you,
because in you, I know the battle is won

I know I have sinned and fallen
short of your precious glory
But no one is perfect, and I thank you for
your grace that I still live to tell my story

You created a purpose for me to serve you
just as you did for your angel, Gabriel
And, I will depend on you, Lord, to fulfill
that purpose because I know you are able

The devil thought he had me, but
in Jesus name he has to let me go
You have spared my life, once again,
and out of my mouth the praises will flow

You have kept me, Lord Jesus; you
have kept me thru another trying day
You have kept me safe from harm
and even wiped all of my tears away

Rayna Stephens

So now Lord, I'm ready! I am
ready to go thru the battle for you
Because as long as your spirit lives
in me, I know you will see me thru

God, I'm nervous, so I need someone I can
trust without a doubt, to be by my side
You're the only 'One' who's perfect, so I
will put all my trust in you to be my guide

August 1, 2009

Rayna Stephens

A Sober Soul

My soul is drunken by heartaches,
despair, anguish and pain
My mind is cloudy; don't know if
the day has brought sunshine or rain

My spiritual vision is blurred and
my soul's equilibrium is off balance
I've lost track of time and it feels as
though I'm losing my spiritual talents

The devil has poisoned me; I've allowed
him to take my precious kingdom gifts away
I want them back but the poison feels so
good and it continues to lead me astray

I say and give unkind responses
that hurt my family and friends
I'm bound in this prison called flesh;
consumed by a countless measure of sin

I've stepped outside the will of God; therefore,
I've stepped outside of my character
I've got to overcome this addiction
because my soul has to get better

Thru this drunken soul, I call on Jesus; because,
with him, I need to have a conversation
Lord, I need you to clean me up and make
me whole again; I need some rehabilitation

God's Words

So, at this very moment, I'll run back into your
powerful hands; I need you to take control
I've been addicted to satan's poison for too
long and, once again, I desire to have a sober soul

March 15, 2011

Rayna Stephens

IDENTITY CRISIS

DO YOU KNOW WHO YOU ARE?
WHAT'S YOUR TRUE IDENTITY?

Is it the expensive clothes that define who you are?
Or, what about the fancy cars and homes that you possess?
Is it the successful job that you acquired underhandedly?
Or, the job that requires you to destroy
people's lives just to make a quick dollar?

DO YOU KNOW WHO YOU ARE?
WHAT'S YOUR TRUE IDENTITY?

Is it the long hair or the
seductive eyes that defines you?
Or, what about the short skirts or booty
shorts that reveals your prize possessions?
Is it the number of men you seduce to
keep your bills paid each month?
Or, is it your money you use to buy a
man's love believing that he will be faithful?

DO YOU KNOW WHO YOUR ARE?
WHAT'S YOUR TRUE IDENTITY?

Is it the five hundred dollar suit and
the Stacy Adam shoes that define you?
Or, is it that fresh haircut and clean
facial trim that the ladies love to see?
Is it the sweet 'nothings' that you whisper
in her ear to get her into your bed?
Or, is it your money that you use to lure
her and to demand power and respect?

**DO YOU KNOW WHO YOU ARE?
WHAT'S YOUR TRUE IDENTITY?**

Is it the fact that we are God's children
and we have dominion over the earth?
Or, is it the fact that we are descendants
of Abraham and heirs of this land?
Is it the rest that we find in our Lord; and
the peace and joy that dwells within our spirit?
Or, it is the fact that we are VICTORIOUS people and
more than conquerors thru our Lord and Savior, Jesus Christ?!

**DO YOU KNOW WHO YOU ARE?
WHAT'S YOUR TRUE IDENTITY?**

June 25, 2009

Rayna Stephens

COME UNTO ME

Come unto me, come on. For you,
I've been waiting patiently;
Knock and you shall receive.

Come unto to me, come on.
Just let me take control;
I will deliver you from
that stronghold.

Come unto to me, come on. I'm
waiting with my arms out stretched;
Ready to save, you, the lost wretch.

Come unto to me, come on.
I'm not going anywhere;
Just want you to try
me if you dare.

Come unto me, come on. I know
you are tired of your worldly ways;
Just call on me so that you may be saved.

Come unto to me, come on. You
said maybe another time and date;
Ok, I'll have mercy, this time; I will wait;
Just make sure that when you come,
it's not too late.

January 4, 2010

HE WILL DELIVER YOU

You don't have to be ashamed
to tell me your story
No one is perfect; we all have
fallen short of God's glory

It doesn't matter to God what
you have said or done
God said that he will save you
thru the blood of his only Son

We all go thru trials and tribulations while in this land
You must believe in yourself; and
know God has the master plan

I'm not trying to preach to you
or even tell you what to do
I'm saying, God said he will deliver
you; and I believe it to be true

So you have to believe Him for yourself
that what he says, he will do
And know that your loved ones will
always be there to pray you thru

January 23, 2010

Rayna Stephens

THE VISIT

I'm lying here in the dark with my
blanket covering me; I can't see,
Oh Lord, who's there? Can't open
my eyes; I feel someone over me.

Oh no! I can't move my body; please
don't say it's over; am I dead?
No wait, I'm still here, but whose
gentle hand is caressing my head?

I feel relaxed, He's speaking to me, but
no words are physically coming out,
I've read about this being; it's got to
be the Holy Spirit, without a doubt.

I asked why was he here; why did
he choose me on this particular night.
He told me that I had asked the Father
for the desires of my heart so he
sent him to make it right.

He told me I asked him to heal, deliver
and bless me with sound direction,
And by His grace, he is here tonight
to make, in me, these corrections.

I told him that first, I want to thank
God, in advance, for what he has done,
I wanted to thank Him for saving
me thru the precious blood of his Son.

God's Words

I wanted to thank Him for being there
when my life was down in the valley,
And I wanted to thank him for sending,
you, the Holy Spirit, to cover me.

He asked me if I had anything else to say
because his ears were attentive to me;
He told me to be still and know that he
is God, so let him fulfill my earnest plea.

I laid still and the Holy Spirit wrapped
himself around me with a gentle squeeze,
I drifted off reassured that my desires
were granted and then I rested in peace.

Without a worry, I gave all my problems
and burdens over to the number 'one' Boss,
Because He has taken care of everyone
of them, when, for me, he died on the Cross!

June 2, 2010

Rayna Stephens

FROM SATAN'S PLAYPEN BACK TO THE GARDEN OF EDEN

The pleasures of the world seem
to have taken control of me;
They have filled my spirit so high
that it's blinding and I can not see;
Why do I feel completely lost with hurt
inside; what is about to become of me?

My frustration outweighs my happiness
and my depression outweighs my joy;
My flesh has taken control of my spirit,
and my sinful nature I seem to enjoy;
I feel as if I'm bound in satan's playpen
and he's tossing me around like a broken toy.

Some days he makes me feel as if I'm
on top of the world until I come crashing down;
He gives me money, cars and clothes to make
me feel like I'm the king who wears the crown;
I feel like I'm the man until I discover
that I'm the disgraceful talk of the town.

He sits back and laughs at me while I'm
angry and confused; sulking in my tears;
He even laughs in disgust when I indulge
in sexual corruption with my peers;
He has built a smokescreen to make
me believe I can't overcome my fears.

Rayna Stephens

Drugs, sex, lies, murder, robbing and
stealing, money and homosexuality;
Now, I realize that I'm indulging in a
careless, destructive ungodly spirituality;
I need someone more powerful to save
my soul and bring me back to reality.

How will I make it; who do I call
on to get me out of this mess?
I heard a small sweet voice say, "I can
deliver you from all of your distress;"
I am the comforter you've always desired
and I guarantee, in me, you will find rest.

I have been your peace, joy, strength
and your love since the beginning of time
Satan had you bound in the flesh and
you would do as he said at the drop of a dime
I knew you would return to me, because
I created you and you have always been mine.

I can save you, but you first have to
believe I died on the cross for all your sins
You must confess with your mouth and
believe in your heart that thru me, you can win
Then, step out on faith and trust that
I will deliver you from satan's playpen.

I did not say your journey thru this
battle would be even pleasurable
You will have moments of frustration and
tears; and it will become uncomfortable
But, if you endure the trial and trust that you
have won, your walk will become desirable

God's Words

So strap up, because you are about to
walk, fiercely, out of satan's playpen
I have equipped you with all the weapons
needed; the weapons from the spirit within
And now you will see I have created a new
thing for you in the Garden of Eden!!!!

June 18, 2009

HAPPY "BIRTH"DAY

Happy birthday to you
To you who has been
bound for so long.
Happy birthday to you
Because now you're free
and living a new song.

Happy birthday to you
To you who never thought
you would be set free.
Happy birthday to you
Because you have finally
learned God's decrees.

Happy birthday to you
To you who has been
under satan's stronghold.
Happy birthday to you
Because you opened your
spirit so God could take control.

Happy birthday to you
To you who has been held
captive in your addictions.
Happy birthday to you
Because you felt weak and overcome
by God's Holy convictions.

Happy birthday to you
To you who thought this
day would never come.
Happy birthday to you
Because you did not
turn back and run.

Happy birthday to you
To you who has been in the
wilderness; scared and lost.
Happy birthday to you
Because now you've been redeemed
by the 'One' who died on the Cross!

HAPPY BIRTHDAY!

July 13, 2009

Rayna Stephens

LIVING IN THE PARADISE OF GOD'S CHARACTER

When I'm awakened by the harmonized
chirps of the beautiful birds
I know you have blessed me with
another day of new grace and mercy.

When I walk outside and feel the gentle
morning breeze whisk across my face
I know it's the sweet and calm
whispers of your loving voice.

When I feel the mid-day heat of the
sun glazing on my delicate skin
I know you're shining down, on
me, your peace and your joy.

When the summer showers pour from
the heavens, soaking me from head to toe
I know your Holy Spirit is
cleansing my soul from within.

When the rainbow appears after the
storm, with many majestic colors
I know you continue to hold to
your promises for my life.

When the sun began to set at the
dusk of day; and the horizon appears
I know your love and faithfulness
reigns from the beginning of time.

God's Words

When the midnight hour has drawn
near and all I can see is the moon
I know you are my light when I walk
thru the valley of the shadow of death.

And when you awaken me, once
again, to repeat the process
I know you had favor on me to live
another day in the Paradise of Your Character.

July 14, 2009

Rayna Stephens

I'VE BEEN KEPT

I've been kept thru the storms and the pouring rain
Been kept thru the heartaches and terrible pain

I've been kept thru my sicknesses and my sorrows
Been kept when I thought there was no tomorrow

I've been kept thru all of my trials and tribulations
Been kept thru my most devastating situations

I've been kept in the darkness of the midnight hour
Been kept by the 'One' with the utmost power

I've been kept thru my stumbling blocks and my stepping stones
Been kept when I thought that all hope was gone

I've been kept thru the tedious journey of parenthood
Been kept when I doubted Him and then knew that He would

I've been kept thru the sweat and the tears of this race
Been kept by my Father's amazing grace

I've been kept thru my life in the good and bad times
Been kept at the very moment that I wrote this rhyme

I've been kept thru the heat of the blazing fire
Been kept by the 'One' who never gets tired

I've been kept when my eyes
were blinded and could not see
Been kept by my Lord and Savior,
Oh thank you, Jesus, for keeping me!

July 10, 2010

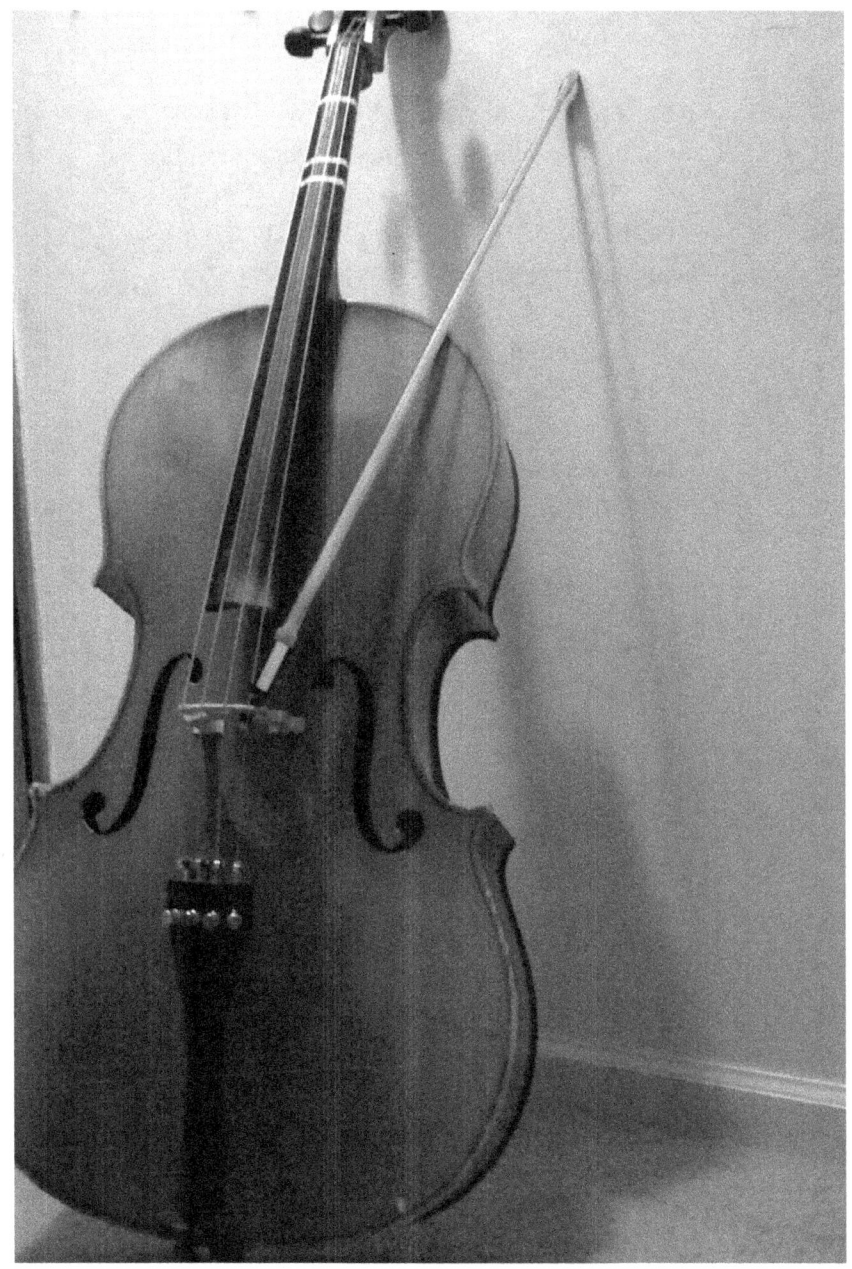

Rayna Stephens

WHO I AM

I am a bright and radiant being who dwells
within the realm of the most Sovereign God.

I am a vibrant, spirit-filled vessel and am
contagious with joy, peace, hope and love.

I am a soldier in the King's army; suited
by His armor and ready for the battle.

I am a tender touch as gracious, merciful
and forgiving as my Father has been to me.

I am a faithful employee of my Father's business; who tarries along
the day, diligently, to provide for her loved ones.

I am a sculpted rib made to fit only one ribcage; and a precious
helpmeet chosen to reverence and honor her 'head'.

I am a rare and beautiful jewel who
is submerged in the land of the Creator.

I AM A VIRTUOUS WOMAN OF CHRIST!

February 19, 2010

True "Model of Beauty"

I was asked what makes a woman a true "model of beauty"
It first starts within; a woman knowing her feminine duty

It's knowing, her innermost precious and valuable worth
It's knowing, her importance and her role on this earth

It's knowing, that using your outer
beauty doesn't always make life simple
It's knowing, that her body is not
just a vessel, but a beautiful temple

"Beauty" is the grace, peace, joy and
love that flow from the inside out
"Model" is the example of what
beauty is really all about

Beauty is not always what you can
put your hands on or physically see
You have to look deeper to see the true
"model of beauty" that is within me!

April 12, 2010

Rayna Stephens

FRIEND

I haven't had a friend like you in quite a while
Who allows me to be me and who makes me smile

Who teaches me the word and God's attributes
And shows concern to me that many do not contribute

Who lends an ear and genuinely listens
And gives godly advice to help me make godly decisions

God is blessing us more than we can realize
See not from the world's view, but thru your spiritual eyes

So thank you for being a good friend indeed
God is always on time and knows exactly what I need

December 01, 2010

Rayna Stephens

MY COMPLIMENT

He's the special man God designed to
compliment my earthly and spiritual life
He's the one who has been longing for
me, his helpmeet; his God-fearing wife

He's the creation that was designed to
accent my strength, character and faith
He was designed to be my spiritual
'head' and to lead me from day to day

He was designed to hold it down,
thru Christ, when times get rough
And to trust God gave him a helpmeet
to assist when the going gets tough

He was designed to have power and
dominion over this gift called Earth
And to admire his woman's beauty; to
know, value and cherish her worth

He was designed to minister to me with
his mind, body and soul, in Jesus name
To pour himself into me so that
we may become one in the same

Yes! He was designed just for me; so I'll
continue to wait patiently for my Heaven sent
And thank you, in advance Lord,
for my husband, my Compliment!

September 23, 2010

A Kingdom Man

Inspired by Rev. Brian Lipscomb

A kingdom man, where can he be found?
How do I know him? What does he
look like? How does he sound?

Where do I go to find him? Will he hear my call?
Are there any kingdom men left? Are there any left at all?

Would I know a kingdom man if I looked him in the face?
Tell me God, am I looking in the right or the wrong place?

Then, you spoke into my spirit that
kingdom men are still around,
You will know when he speaks: his inner
voice will have a Christ-like sound.

His walk with Christ will display
strength whether he has won or lost,
His character will honor God in
truth, no matter what the cost.

His spirit will reverence the
Father in such a God-fearing way,
You would not want to leave his
presence; you will always want to stay.

You will admire him for the respect that he has for himself,
You will be amazed at the respect that he has for everyone else.

Rayna Stephens

        You will know a kingdom man because
          he will love with the love of Christ
          He will wait to become 'one' with
            you; until you become his wife.

        So wait, my Queen, wait on me; I have
          this union in the palm of my hand
       And in due season, you won't have to look;
     because I will deliver to you, a Kingdom Man!

                December 2, 2010

MISSING RIB

Who's your missing rib?
She is the 'one', who can complete
your sentences and your thoughts,
She is so deeply in love with you
that she doesn't dwell on your faults.

She is the 'one', who will hold
you up when you can't hold yourself,
She desires to serve and put you
first before she puts herself.

Who's your missing rib?
She is the 'one', who is humble and wise
enough to honor and reverence you,
She doesn't mind submitting
herself and being obedient to you.
She is the 'one' who is discreet, respectful,
chaste, and a keeper of your home,
She always remind you that she
only wants you; and you alone

Who's your missing rib?
She is the 'one' who fills you with reassurance
and makes you feel on top of the world
She makes you feel, without a doubt,
you can confidently say' That's my Girl!'

Rayna Stephens

She is the 'one' who completes and
serves with you in the body of Christ
She will always be there for you, faithfully,
thru the good and bad times in your life.

So tell me, who's your missing rib?

March 19, 2010

A Kingdom Woman

A kingdom woman walks with
confidence, strength, wisdom and finesse;
She has balance in her life's duties:
family, friends, business and rest.

A kingdom woman can speak to
you without saying one word;
She speaks thru the spirit; and
by your heart, you have heard.

A kingdom woman's spirit is
humble, caring, nurturing and gentle;
Her touch is soothing, reassuring, healing and sensual.

A kingdom woman loves with her heart
and soul; she loves without a limit;
Her love is never harsh, cruel,
deceitful, selfish or timid.

A kingdom woman treats her children
as true gifts that God has given to her;
She feels blessed to be chosen for
the opportunity of being their mother.

A kingdom woman's love is unconditional
thru the love of Jesus Christ;
She desires to pour out her Heavenly
passion into her husband, as his kingdom wife.

Rayna Stephens

A kingdom woman reverences, honors,
and glorifies her Lord and Savior;
She worships and praises Him,
everyday, for his unmerited favor.

A kingdom woman steps out on faith
each day she is faithfully awakened;
She believes on God's word for
every spiritual step she has taken.

A kingdom woman is not perfect
but strives to live a righteous life;
She may fall sometimes, but she picks
herself up and gets back in the fight.

A kingdom woman, are there any left?
If she looked you in the face, would you know?
So when you have found your kingdom woman,
be sure to hold her close and never her let go!

April 6, 2011

I'M READY

I'm ready for this journey called marriage;
ready for the ups and the downs;
Ready for the trials that will tempt me to turn
back; but I'm strong now, I won't turn around.

I'm ready for my Heaven sent husband;
ready for my precious kingdom man;
Ready to go thru the battle with him;
by his side I will faithfully stand.

I'm ready for the pain, prayers,
longsuffering, the tears and frustrations;
Ready for the faith, joy, love, peace,
determination and patience.

I'm ready to walk thru the fire, with him;
armed and equipped with God's Holy word;
Ready to trust the spirit within him; no
matter what hatred is felt or lies that is heard.

I'm ready to encourage him, support him and
build him up to do God's Kingdom work;
Ready to see him take back what God has
ordained for us and that is dominion over the earth.

I'm ready to service him with submission, honor,
reverence and obedience as worship to Christ,
Ready for his love, respect, protection and
honor that he will give to me as his wife.

Rayna Stephens

> I'm ready for this union I thought would
> never happen but God said "Yes," instead,
> Ready for the love of my life, my soul mate,
> my kingdom man, my "SPIRITUAL HEAD!"

> January 12, 2011

HAVE YOUR WAY

Have your way with me, oh Lord;
I now know who sits on the throne
Do with me as you please; I desire
   to live in your will, not my own

I know you are compassionate and
gracious; I know you are fair and just
I know you will correct me when I'm
   wrong, so please do so, if you must

Consume me, use me and direct
   my path; it is your face that I seek
Shut my being down, and thru this
   vessel allow the Holy Spirit to speak

Have your way with me, oh Lord; it was
   by your grace that my life was spared
I'll do what you want me to; I know you
   wouldn't give me more than I could bare

Tell me where to go and what to
   do, and I'll do it; for you I will obey
Give me wisdom and discernment to
   say to others what you want me to say

Have your way with me, oh Lord; I know,
   sometimes, this journey will not be easy
But I'm not worried, not even a little,
   because I know that you are carrying me

Rayna Stephens

>Have your way with me, oh Lord;
>your way will never steer me wrong
>I desire to sit at your feet to worship
>and praise you all the day long
>
>Have your way with me, oh Lord; I
>now know who sits on the throne
>I desire to be in that number when you
>come, again, to take your children home

>March 25, 2010

God's Words

Rayna Stephens

PERSEVERE

Inspired by, my daughter, Chantrelle

When all else fails, you can count on Thee
When you feel all alone in the dark
He will be all the light that you need to see.

It's not always easy to make the right decision in life
But if you struggle and strive and don't give up on God
I'm a living witness that He will make everything alright.

So wipe your tears and dry your eyes,
this is a new beginning for you
Stay in the fight, persevere and

keep the faith no matter what
And watch how everything you do,
in Christ, will began to manifest and bloom!

March 2009

STEPPING INTO MY DESTINY

You said that on this tedious
journey, I may have missed a step,
Maybe I should have turned
right instead of turning left.

You said my mind may be idle which
leaves room for satan to walk in,
And, maybe now is not the time for
me to fulfill my desires from within.

You said that maybe there's a career
waiting for me to come and get,
But, because I've missed a step and was
looking for something else; to it, I cannot connect.

But God said he was going to take me
on a journey that I may not understand,
Because he has something much
greater for me; He has the master plan.

And on this journey, he will have
many complex jobs for me to do,
I shouldn't worry how I will complete
the task; He'll be the 'One' to carry me thru.

He said the world will not understand
how I am surviving from day to day,
And he wanted me to hold fast to his
word no matter what they do or say.

Rayna Stephens

I will never leave or forsake you while
on this faith walk, is what he said to me,
And I must believe in his sovereign powers
while walking this spiritual journey.

And when I look back over all my
trials while taking this walk with thee,
I will see that those trials were only
the steps leading into my destiny!

November 30, 2010

ON THE OUTSIDE TRYING TO LOOK IN

Inspired by, my son, Jamon

You, who's on the outside, trying to
look in; tell me, what do you see?
Do you see the righteous truth or
just what you assumed it to be?

Do you see the anointing that has
been manifested in my dwelling?
Or have you written your own story
about me; and is it lies that you're telling?

Do you see the peace that God has
given to me in the midst of my storm?
Or have you assumed there's no way I could
feel peace because my trial is beyond the norm?

Do you see the joy that overflows out
of me; joy unspeakable joy?
Or have you assumed that my Heavenly
happiness is only a cover-up; a decoy?

Do you see the genuine love that flows
from one spirit to another in this place?
Or have you assumed that my love isn't real
and I'm hiding it with a fake smile on my face?

Do you see the faith that I have in the
Lord, thru my trials, to be extraordinary?
Or have you assumed I've put my trust in something
else because my assignment is out of the ordinary?

Rayna Stephens

Do you see the endurance that God has
graciously bestowed upon me to prevail?
Or have you assumed that I'm not walking
in his will; therefore, my plans will fail?

Do you see the unmerited favor that
God has surrounded me within?
Oh, I forgot, probably not; because
you're on the outside trying to look in!

December 9, 2010

CONFIDENCE IN CHRIST

This is the confidence, Lord Jesus,
which we humbly have in you,
That if we ask and believe; we know
you will faithfully see us thru.

Providing us with a miraculous
and powerful breakthru,
Because you're God and God all by
yourself and that is what you do.

Comforting us thru our sufferings
and our painful trials,
Reminding us that you're our
keeper and the 'One' we can rely on.

You knew our future and destiny
before we were ever conceived,
And if we practice the faith you have given
to us, our blessings we may humbly receive.

Father, our confidence is in you, knowing
you will do what we ask, if only we believe,
So thank you, Jesus, for being my strength;
for reassuring me that you would never leave.

I need you, oh Lord, to come thru for
me; oh Lord, I need you right now,
I can't even fathom how you will do it,
but I know you will do it for me, somehow.

Rayna Stephens

You said no one could get to the
Father unless they first come thru you,
I desire to see my Father's kingdom; so
I'm asking you to please carry me thru.

Keep me, oh Lord, according to
your will, in everything that I do,
Because when it's all over, said and
done, all glory and honor belongs to you.

So this is the confidence, Lord Jesus,
which we so humbly have in you,
That if we ask you and then believe;
we know you will faithfully see us thru.

February 11, 2011

I Won With a Bad Hand

My life was dealt a bad hand and I was counted
out by some of my family and so-called friends
But, there was a man named Jesus who
washed away and forgave me of all my sins
He came and cleansed me; made me
a better person; made me whole again

He purified my heart and took away
all of the dirt, grime and cruddy stains
He refreshed my mind and my
thoughts and gave to me a new name
Huh! It looks to me that even with this
bad hand I was dealt, I'm still in the game

He restored my bruised and
misused body back to its beginning
He has given me true love and respect for
myself; not to use this temple for sinning
He has given me wisdom, discernment, and faith;
now that sounds like a hand with a chance of winning

He has given me courage and determination
to play this bad hand with confidence
Believing the **only** good card I hold in my
hand, which is Jesus, will be my reassurance
Now the enemy thought he had control; he's doubting
his hand and questioning his own intelligence

Rayna Stephens

It's time to play the last card; the Jesus card; my
faith has kicked in and the final round has begun
I believe what God has promised to me, thru
our Savior, Jesus Christ, His only begotten Son
And out of the bad hand I was dealt, the Jesus card was all
I needed, because with Him, the game was already won!

April 23, 2010

FAITHFULNESS IN MY FAITH

I continue to believe so my
blessings I may receive
I continue to believe; not this
time satan; I won't be deceived

I continue to pray for my
strength to keep the faith
I continue to pray; no satan;
there's nothing you can do or say

I continue to meditate so I
may stay focused on You
I continue to meditate; flee from me
satan; you've lost the battle, you're thru

I continue in obedience because
that's what I'm required to do
I continue in obedience; give it
up satan; I don't belong to you

I continue in grace because
God has favor over my life
I continue in grace; you're on your own
now, satan; deal with your own strife

I continue in mercy because
of God's unconditional love
I continue in mercy; it's your fault, satan,
you were kicked out of heaven above

Rayna Stephens

> I continue in compassion because
> God cares so much for me
> I continue in compassion; satan,
> you no longer have control over me
>
> I continue in love because He
> died on the Cross for you and I
> I continue in love; my last comment
> to you, satan; the devil is a LIE
>
> April 12, 2010

God's Words

Rayna Stephens

WORSHIP

I worship you, oh Lord,
for all of your beatitudes
I humbly bow down to you
to show you my gratitude

I worship you, oh Lord,
because of your attributes
I praise you for all the blessings,
in my life that you contribute

I worship you, oh Lord, for leaving me
a comforter called the Holy Spirit
I honor you for giving me wisdom
and discernment to hear it

I worship you, oh Lord,
because of your Holiness
I adore you for allowing
me to feel your closeness

I worship you, oh Lord,
because you are righteous
I obey you so grief will
not fill my conscience

I worship you, oh Lord,
because of your Sovereignty
I reverence you as you show me
your powers; they are so mighty

God's Words

I worship you, oh Lord,
because of your unmerited favor
I thank you for mercy and forgiveness
that comes from our Lord and Savior

I worship you, oh Lord, because
you are the keeper of my soul
I appreciate you continuously cleansing
me from sin so I may be whole

I worship you, oh Lord, for giving
me your only begotten Son, Jesus
I magnify Him for surrendering
his life on the cross for us

I worship you, oh Lord,
because of your sacred love
I love you dearly and thank you for
everything that comes from the Kingdom above

I worship you, oh Lord, just
because of who you are
I glorify you, Father; for you are my
light in darkness; my shining star

March 13, 2011

Rayna Stephens

A Balm Thru the Storm

I'm coming out of this
vicious storm head strong
I'm letting God guide me
so I won't be steered wrong

The season in the eye of the
storm was peaceful and calm
But walking thru the storm,
I discovered I needed a balm

A balm to heal my frustrations,
anger and discouragements
And to fill me with joy, peace,
faith, forgiveness and encouragement

A balm to reassure me that
everything would be alright
Even if I can't see my blessings
thru this human eye sight

A balm to hold me up thru
the storm as I am falling
And to give me strength thru
the storm even when I'm crawling

A balm to mold me, make me,
shape me and recreate me
So that thru the storm, the
Christ in me, others would see

Rayna Stephens

A balm to build, in me, divine
character and determination
So that I may be a testimony, not
just to one, but to many nations

A balm to manifest within
my spirit a brand new thing
So that a new life I may live
and a new song I may sing

A balm to show me nothing is
impossible for him; He's the 'One'
Because He rose with all power
in his hands; He's the 'Son'

You told me thru this storm,
in You, I would find rest
Now, it's time for my miraculous
blessings because I have stood the test

So thank you, Jesus, for being my
strength and my healing balm
And thank you for carrying and
protecting me thru this vicious storm

September 9, 2009

God's Words

FEAR INTO FAITH

Inspired by Andrea Watson-Harris

Hello God, it's me, wondering how I can turn my fear into faith.
How do I do it, God; where do I start; what do I say?
Please Lord Jesus, help me turn my fear into faith.

I hear you my child; your prayers are
answered, and I will teach you, starting today;
I will show you a miracle that will
leave you amazed, not knowing what to say;
And this will be the beginning of your
journey of turning your fear into faith.

I will show you how you were and what you use to do;
When you thought no one was there;
I was the 'One' who kept you;
I kept you from the dangers of yourself;
yes, I brought you safely thru.

All the times you couldn't pay your bills
and became scared out of your mind;
You worried and cried, you were frustrated
and angry; yet, I came thru for you on time;
You didn't say thank you, but I forgave you
and would do it, again, at the drop of a dime.

When you were lonely and depressed
and had no one there to hold you;
I was always there showing my
compassion, comforting and consoling you;
Why do you think you are strengthened,
revived and have joy in you?

Rayna Stephens

When you were walking thru storms
and you felt there was no way out;
It was me who was there to guide and
teach you what life was really about;
Once again, I was right there to sustain
you because I love you without a doubt.

So stop wondering how to turn your fear
into faith, because faith you had all along;
You just call on me, rest in me, and thank
me in advance for making your faith strong;
And watch how I turn your fear into faith
and manifest, in you, a brand new song!

March 19, 2010

I Believe

I believe what you speak
into my spirit to be true
I believe what you say you
will do, you **are** going to do.

I believe you are not just holding
my hand, but you're carrying me
I believe you're taking me into my
season, even if my season I cannot see.

I believe you have given me
reassurance, thru your word, to hold fast
I believe no matter how satan tries to stop
your plans; those plans **will** come to pass.

I believe you are using me as your vessel
to show and tell others about what you can do
And I believe they will desire the same spirit
that is within me; and that is the spirit of **You!**

March 18, 2010

Rayna Stephens

FAITH WALK

You asked me to bless
you in a mighty way;
But are you truly ready
for me to test your faith?

Are you ready for the hurt
and pain; sorrow and tears?
Are you ready to endure for days,
months, and sometimes even years?

Will you trust me to break you
and put you into the scorching fire?
So I may purify your soul in
order to take you higher?

Are you ready for me to mold,
shape and restore your heart?
Are you willing to draw closer to me and
build a relationship that will never part?

Are you ready to step off the cliff, not
knowing what you're about to step into?
Will you trust that when you feel like you're
falling; my hand is already there to catch you?

Will you trust that everything I
say and do will come to pass?
Or will you believe in the world's view
that is temporary and will not last?

God's Words

Will you allow me to manifest in
you wisdom, joy, hope, love and peace;
So when you have walked thru your storm,
these treasures you have won will never cease?

Will you believe in the physical eye; what
the world says and only what you can see?
Or will you believe in the spiritual eye,
what's not in front of you, believing in me?

Will you trust I am taking you thru the storm,
not to harm you, but to prepare you for my kingdom?
So when you stand in front of me on
judgment day, I may say, servant well done?

Will you believe that I am the God of all
creation, or will you give up and say I'm all talk?
Or will you trust me with your heart, mind,
and soul; and take, with me, this faith walk?!

March 4, 2010

ABOUT THE AUTHOR

Rayna Roxanne is a strong soldier in the army of the Lord who is totally devoted to uplifting the body of Jesus Christ and advancing the Kingdom of God throughout the earth. God has equipped her with many gifts and talents that help her reach the world one soul at a time.

I am thankful that divine intervention brought us together for a purpose greater than ourselves. I have been blessed to know Rayna for over two decades; and from the moment we met, I knew that there was something special about her. We were both so young, barely in the eighth grade and from such different worlds. Through her smile, her exterior was rough and defensive. It was obvious that she had grown up fighting and constantly protecting herself. She was a very bright student and I admired how Math and English curriculums came effortlessly to her.

Like most adolescents, she felt misunderstood; she was lost. I remember, feeling as if she was missing the crucial support needed for her development from a girl to a young lady. She knew a lot; those big beautiful eyes had seen too much in a short time. On the opposite end, I had grown up very sheltered. My parents were very busy and loving pastors; and what Rayna knew intrigued me. It was so different from what I had always known. She was a survivor with a deep longing to feel special and know the unconditional love of Jesus Christ.

Throughout the years we have made many mistakes together. We have developed into God fearing women with ministries and a passion for the will of God. I will never forget how we have lost, loved, learned, prayed, and felt great pain together. We also rejoiced, laughed, cooked, and cried, then, laughed some more, together!! Amazingly, through it all we have remained unconditional friends. And we will glorify God and WIN together. **1 Chronicles 29:11** says: Yours, O Lord, is the greatness and the power and the glory and the victory and the majesty, for all that is in the heavens and in the earth is yours. Yours is the kingdom, O Lord, and you are exalted as head above all.

God has a way of giving you enough of what you need so that there is plenty to give to others. Rayna has a gift of touching the hearts of others with honesty and by walking in the spirit of love. **1 Thessalonians 3:12** says: And may the Lord make you increase and abound in love for one another and for all, as we do for you. Her poetry will reach the world right where they are, and with plain and simple words so that all may understand.

Rayna is originally from Little Rock, Arkansas and currently resides in Atlanta, Georgia where she has been a resident for five years. She is a wonderful mother of four beautiful children and one energetic grandchild. They are all unique and require individual attention, yet, she finds a way to make them all feel special and loved. Her children will soon rise up and call her blessed. I feel extremely blessed to call her my friend.

-Bethany Devine-

Rayna Stephens

God has blessed my son, Jamon Stephens, to have a ministry in writing, as well. As he grows and mature, he too, shall have a book of poetic praises to our Father!

A sample of his work:

A Poem for the Youth

Look around, what have we become?
Pregnancy, drugs, gangs and guns.

It seems as though we have forgotten who we are
A child of God, a shining light, a star.

We must not forget that we make up the body of the Lord
And when the time comes, we too,
will be judged by His righteous sword.

It pains me to see how far the children have fled away
They have fallen subject to satin, who's
constantly leading them astray.

But it's not the end, my dear friend, the battle has just begun
We have another chance because of the death of the Holy Son.

God said: Suffer the little children
unto me and do not hinder them;
for the kingdom of God belongs to such as these
So pray to Him for forgiveness; it's just that simple, you see.

As the youth, we are going to have
struggles, hard times and temptations
But once we overcome, boy, oh boy,
there will be a jubilant revelation!

April 12, 2010

Rayna Stephens

I am dedicating this book to a dear friend and sister in Christ, Nicola Williams, who passed away in September 2004 of cancer; leaving behind three beautiful children (Shandrika, Jessica and Nicolas) whom are my god children. Her daughter, Jessica, wrote a poem in remembrance of her mother. We will meet again someday. With Love.....Ray

My Mother

My mother is as sweet as strawberries;
the sweetness goes around
But, one day, we had to put her in the ground

I have not told what I need to
because no one really knows
Not my family, my friends or even my foes

I don't know what to say because it is hard, where do I start?
I pretend nothing is wrong when I'm missing her in my heart

Yes, I know my mother is gone and will never come back
But, we will meet again, this I know for a fact

She will never again have to leave
I'll have someone to hug and believe in me

She will hold me, and love
me and tell me good night
And everything will finally be alright

My mother, my dearest friend
We soon will be together again

I love you dearly and miss you too
But I know you had to go
when God wanted you.

Jessica Minor-

ORDER INFORMATION

Second Book: Moving Into the New Me
...By Faith!

Order on author's website at:
www.authorraynastephens.com

Author's Contact Information:
Email: info@authorraynastephens.com

www.ingramcontent.com/pod-product-compliance
Lightning Source LLC
Chambersburg PA
CBHW071411290426
44108CB00014B/1774